Teaching English Through Art

by

Sharon Jeffus

Copyright 1994
Revised 2006

ISBN 0-9677386-5-2

The earliest writings of man were visual symbols or pictographs. Communicating takes the shape of the written word and the visual picture. It is very important for students to see the connection and be able to communicate their own ideas. That is the purpose of this book.

A Writing Portfolio

The primary goal of this book is to enable each student to have his or her own writing portfolio. If you wanted to become an artist, you would save your best work to show someone what you can do. In art, you save your student's work in a portfolio because a good portfolio is important in obtaining a job or getting into certain colleges. A good writing portfolio is also important to show someone what you can do. You may want to take this portfolio to your local paper and show the editor some of your samples. Some colleges may want to see samples of your writing prior to your admission. A neat, well organized portfolio is a great asset for any student.

The content of this portfolio is primarily aimed at students grades four through nine, although projects could be modified for other ages. This is an excellent guide for older students who would like to know what to save in a portfolio and gives a good assessment of a student's overall ability in writing. Some of the successful art activities in this book also are appropriate for the student's art portfolio.

Each portfolio should contain:
1. Autobiography or biography; this should be three to five pages typed.
2. Poetry samples; this may include a ballad, a limerick, haiku etc.
3. You need to have a sample of each kind of paragraph including a narrative, persuasive, descriptive, and expository.
4. Essay; you need to have an essay on the topic the student chooses.
5. Character sketch
6. Journal entry
7. Two short stories; this should be the best quality of the student's writing. Some suggestions are mystery, science fiction, adventure, romance, etc. The story should be four to five typewritten pages.
8. A research paper; this needs to be five to eight typewritten pages. It needs to include footnotes and a bibliography with at least three documented sources.

Measurable Goals

Following is a list of measurable goals for your children in their writing skills. Use this checklist for evaluation.

1. I can use interesting vocabulary words.
2. I can write sentences that are not run-ons.
3. I can write exclamatory, declarative, imperative, and interrogative sentences.
4. I can write a paragraph using a good topic sentence, supporting facts, and an interesting ending.
5. I understand the difference between fiction and nonfiction and can write either.
6. I can plan an outline before I write a paper.
7. I can write a character sketch.
8. I can understand and write all the elements of a story.
9. I can write a dialogue into my story and can use correct punctuation.
10. I can write a friendly letter.
11. I can write a business letter.
12. I can write poetry.
13. I understand plot and can write a story with an interesting beginning, middle, and end.
14. I understand the point of view.
15. I can discuss the theme of a story.
16. I can write paragraphs that are narrative, expository, descriptive, and persuasive.
17. I can recognize and write different types of stories.
18. I can recognize and write different forms of propaganda.
19. I understand figurative language.
20. I can write newspaper articles and other forms of nonfiction in an interesting manner.

Descriptive Words

Learning to use descriptive words is an important component of learning how to write creatively. You can actually paint a picture of someone or something using words. On the following pages and below are exercises in using words correctly and creatively to make writing more exciting.

Draw pictures of the following sentences. Did the writer give you a picture in your mind of what the sentence is about?

The deer danced with the spotted dog.

The tall, slim cowboy sat slouched over on his spotted horse.

The graceful ballerina in the shimmering gown glided across the stage.

The garden of daisies and tulips was visited by an army of bees.

WORDS THAT DESCRIBE FEELINGS

Look at the words below. These are words that describe feelings.
Put one of these words under each picture on the following page.
Now use the blank page to draw your own expressions. Put words
under the pictures that describe the expressions on the faces.

aggressive
happy
bashful
disappointed
excited
helpless
interested
stubborn
negative
sorry
cautious
discouraged
exhausted
jealous
relieved
surprised
sad
loved
satisfied
frightened
confused
curious
hurt
lovestruck
shy
undecided
ecstatic
determined
enthusiastic
innocent

EMOTIONS

EMOTIONS

Posters

There are lots of fun ways to learn descriptive words. One is to make a wanted poster with the describing words on the poster. Making letters look like the word is also a good exercise to remember the meaning of the word. A poster is bold and simple in design. You want all the lettering to be easy to read. Look at the poster below. You could choose the topic of a perfect house, or a perfect vacation. Pictures and words communicate ideas. Have you ever heard anyone say, "Do I have to paint you a picture?" Make a wanted poster.

WANTED

THE PERFECT NANNY:

KIND
INTELLIGENT
WITTY
LOVING
GOOD COOK

GOOD DRIVER
LOVES OUTDOORS
LOVES CHILDREN
MUSICIAN
ARTIST

WANTED

Coloring With Words

Look at the following color wheel. Red, yellow, and blue are the primary colors. Between them are the secondary colors: orange, green, and violet. Color the color wheel. Now draw a picture of something that you love that is one particular color. After the picture is finished, write a limerick about the color and the object. In a limerick the rhyme scheme is usually a-a-b-b--a . the first and second line usually rhyme. The third and fourth line usually rhyme. The last line rhymes with the first and second line.

Here is an example:

The pickles were totally green,
They were the largest that I've ever seen,
When you're ready to pucker,
Then you couldn't be luckier,
To eat only pickles not beans!

Colors opposite each other on the color wheel are complementary colors. You can shade the green pickle above with the color red. You can shade a red apple with green. You can shade a yellow banana with violet and an orange with blue. Draw each of these fruits and shade with the complement.

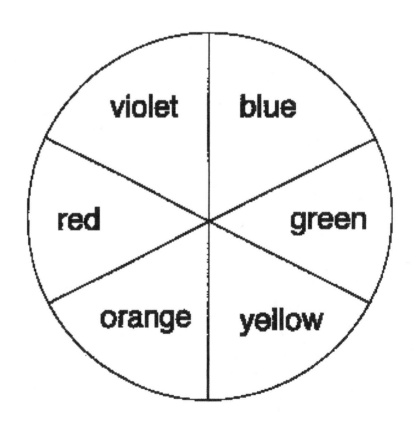

Writing a Color Story

Now that students have been introduced to the color wheel, they are going to write a color story. Have your students use a note pad and go for a walk. They should jot down all the things they see that are one particular color and then when they come home, they need to use them in a story. The color should also be mentioned in the title of the story. Look at the picture above and have the students guess what colors would be in the picture. Hot colors are red, orange and yellow. Cool colors are green, blue and purple. Have students choose which group of colors they would use in the above picture. Would either of the choices change the mood of the picture?

All About Me

A good way to learn descriptive words is to draw a self -portrait of you using the proportions given. Use colors that are expressive of how you feel about you. A collage is a number of various parts being put together into a whole for a unified effect. Use several magazines (with permission) and cut out different words and things that remind you of you. Now glue them around the picture you have drawn. You have a collage. Use just three of those descriptive words in a sentence about you.

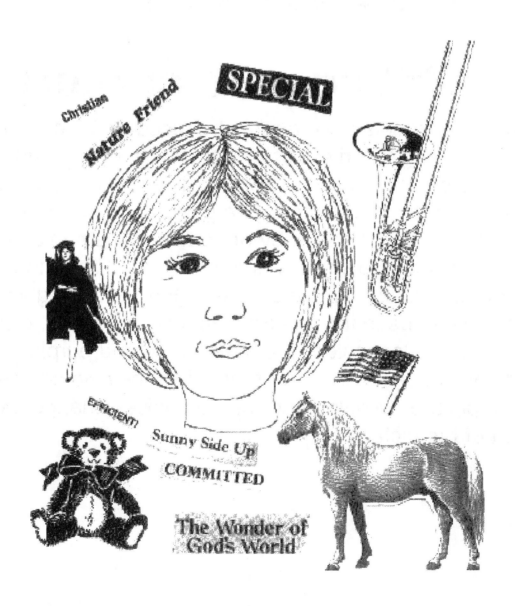

DRAWING THE FACE
IN PROPORTION

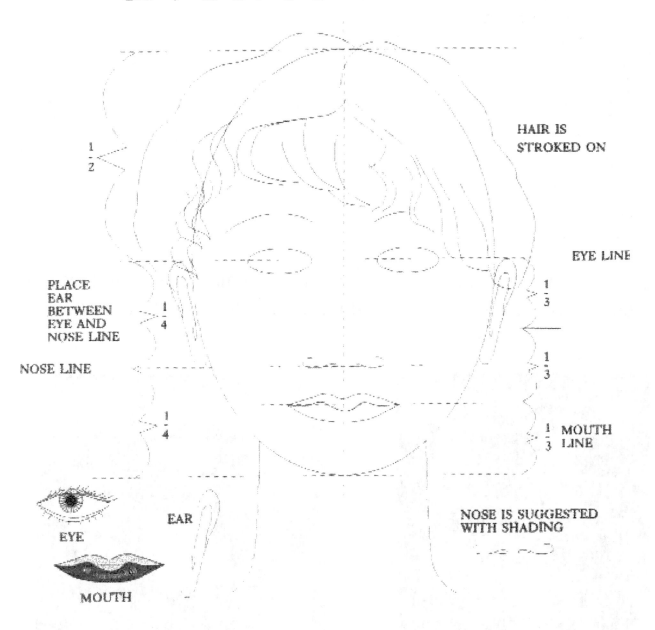

HAIR IS
STROKED ON

$\frac{1}{2}$

EYE LINE

$\frac{1}{3}$

PLACE
EAR
BETWEEN
EYE AND
NOSE LINE

$\frac{1}{4}$

$\frac{1}{3}$

NOSE LINE

$\frac{1}{4}$

$\frac{1}{3}$ MOUTH
LINE

EYE

EAR

NOSE IS SUGGESTED
WITH SHADING

MOUTH

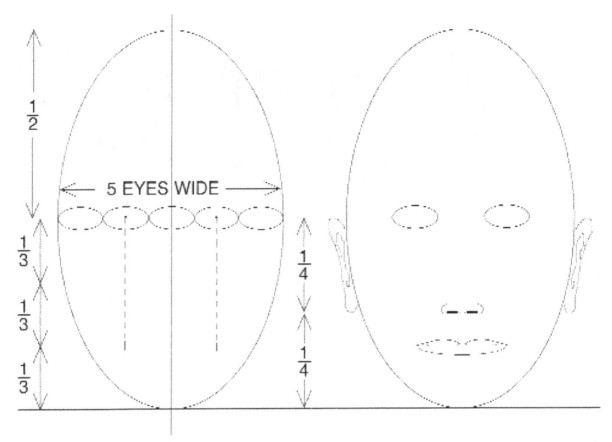

The pictures above and below, show how to make a face in the right proportions. Draw your face and put descriptive words around it.

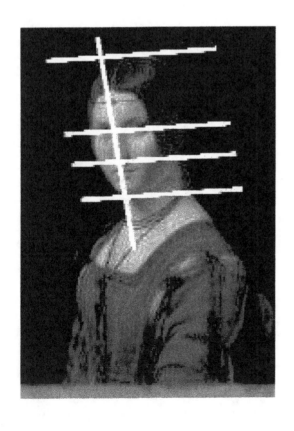

The Nose

Cyrano De Bergerac was the French poet who had a play written about him.   The author of the play is Edmuond Rostand. Cyrano was an intelligent, talented man of reckless bravery. The play is about his love for a beautiful woman.

Cyrano had a very large nose and didn't believe the woman he loved would love him because he considered himself very ugly. He wrote beautiful poetry and allowed another man to read it because he was very shy. The woman fell in love with Cyrano not for what he looked like, but for what he was inside. We all want to be loved for ourselves. Here is an assignment that will be quite a challenge. Design a nose that you could wear for one hour. You might make this nose out of a paper cup. Or you might decide to make it out of a cone. Make sure you can tie it on your face and actually wear it. Now do some things you usually do around the house . Try to eat with your nose on. Maybe you can do exercises. Get the feel of what it is like to have a large nose. Now write a paragraph on what it is like to have a big nose. Did it change you inside to have a large nose? Sometimes there are things about our appearance that make us feel different, but we are the same inside, and it is our inner qualities that count!

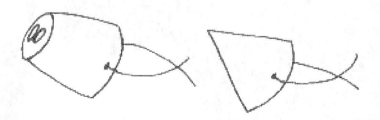

Personification

Personification is a type of figurative language. Personification is when you take an inanimate object and put human characteristics to it. Many Disney cartoons use personification of inanimate objects. The flying carpet in "Aladdin" is an example of personification. The tea cup in "Beauty and the Beast" is another example of personification. Choose an object from around the house. You can use a broom, chair or a plate, or any other object. Make a comic drawing of the object; giving it eyes , a nose, a mouth, etc. Describe your drawing with words in a descriptive paragraph. Now take a picture of flowers, (see example) and turn them into people, giving them human characteristics. Are they shy, or bold?

Similies and Metaphors

A simile is a comparison of two different things using like or as.

Similies and Metaphors

A BUTTERFLY IS LIKE A FLYING FLOWER. This is a simile.
Look at the picture of this simile:

The frog jumped like a bouncing ball.
can you illustrate this simile?

A metaphor is a comparison of two different things <u>without</u> using a word of comparison (like or as).

DAVID WAS A ROCK OF STRENGTH BEFORE THE MIGHTY GOLIATH.

Look at the picture of this metaphor.

The flower was sunshine to the sick child.
Can you illustrate this metaphor?

Look at the picture on the following page and write a simile and a metaphor about it.

Write a sentence using a simile about the picture above. What can
you compare the light to? Now write a metaphor.
In art, the black is **negative space** and the light is **positive space.**

Conjunctions

When I think of a conjunction, I think of a bridge. Look at this picture of the Brooklyn Bridge. It connects two separate pieces of land. A conjunction is a word used to connect words, phrases, clauses, or sentences. They can be coordinating such as **and**, **but**, and **or**. They may be subordinating such as **if, because, though, as,** or **when.** They may be correlative such as: **either.......or, or but.......and**. Make a sentence with a conjunction.

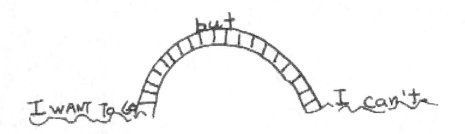

Good Story Words

Putting together words, sentences, and paragraphs correctly will enable you to tell a story with in an effective way. The picture below tells a story visually. List descriptive words you could use about this picture. If you were going to write a story about this picture, what would the title be?

Creating a Mood With Words

Look at the picture below. Can you create in words what this artist has created in pictures? What are some words you can use to describe this picture?

Mood can also be created in colors. If you want to create a dull or dark mood, use neutral colors. Blacks browns and grays create this. Bright colors, especially warm colors create a bright and energetic mood. Cool colors tend to create a calm and lovely mood. What colors would you use in the picture below? Think of 10 mood capturing words and use them in a paragraph to describe this scene.

_____
_____
_____
_____
_____
_____
_____
_____
_____
_____
_____
_____
_____
_____
_____
_____
_____
_____
_____
_____

Kinds of Sentences

There are four kinds of sentence. Interrogative asks a question. Exclamatory shows excitement. Declarative makes a statement. Imperative gives a command. On the following two pages are examples of drawing the sentence with a comic drawing. Fill in the blank places and picture your sentence.

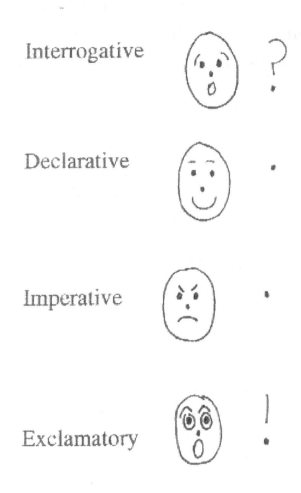

Interrogative

Declarative

Imperative

Exclamatory

Make a cartoon drawing of your favorite character using each of the four different types of sentences.

DECLARATIVE

EXCLAMATORY

INTERROGATIVE

IMPERATIVE

DECLARATIVE

EXCLAMATORY

INTERROGATIVE

IMPERATIVE

An Oxymoron

This is a literary technique in which two contradictory words come together and create a special effect.

jumbo shrimp

tiny the whale

old news

painless dentistry

honest politician

slow lightning

diet chocolate cake

dry water

helpful gossip

Can you draw a picture of an oxymoron? Now use one in a sentence.

Hyperbole

This is an overstatement or exaggeration used for emphasis.

My mom had a cow when she saw the kitchen.

John's eyes popped out when Julie walked in.

Josh hit the ball into the next time zone.

Her dad drove so slow that he was often passed by snails.

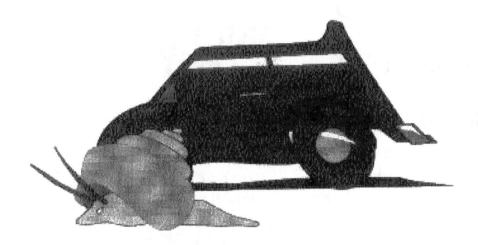

His beard was so long that if the wind was right it would get to town three days before the rest of him.

Can you draw a picture using a hyperbole? Now use hyperbole in a sentence.

Adjectives

The two most important parts of speech are nouns and verbs. An adjective is a word that tells about a noun. It can describe how something looks, feels, tastes, and sounds. It adds interest to our sentence. In most cases adjectives are very easy to find because they are next to the noun. If the adjective isn't next to the noun, just ask yourself if any words in the sentence describe the noun. You can line up adjectives beside each other as long as you use a comma in between each one.

Look at the following pictures. One adjective is already beside the picture. You need to think of three more. Put on your thinking cap and think of a word that describes the person, place, or thing in the picture. Be sure it is an adjective.

small

_____

_____

_____

beautiful

_____

_____

_____

Adverbs

An adverb is a descriptive word. It can modify an adjective, a verb, or another adverb. An adverb tells how, when, where, why, how often, and how much. Adverbs also end in "ly"---but not always. Words like quite, very, and always are adverbs, too. Adverbs of time will tell when, how long, and how often. Adverbs of degree tell how much or how little. Look at the following pictures. Beside each picture is an example of the verb and describing adverb. Fill in the other three examples.

swiftly

_____

_____

_____

happily

_____

_____

_____

An Interjection

Wow! Now this is exciting! An interjection expresses strong emotion or surprise. A comma or explanation mark separates it from the rest of the sentence. Can you make an interjection look like what the word means? Choose a word from the following and then make it look like the word.

Wow! Ouch! Negative! Radical!

Hey! Yeeow! **Wait!** Stop! Go! Yum!

Unbelievable!   Impossible!

Verbs and Adverbs

In this assignment, the student will learn how to use verbs and adverbs more effectively.

First we will talk about a girl going down the street . How many ways can you say this? We will try to say this in five ways. We will use an adverb and a verb in each sentence.

1. The girl hopped quickly down the street.

2. The girl, flinging her arms everywhere, ran wildly down the street.

3. The girl walked very slowly down the street.

4. The girl weakly crawled down the street.

5. The girl energetically bounced a ball down the street.

Look at the sample illustrations of the sentences in the boxes below.

Write and illustrate five sentences using a verb and an adverb in the boxes on the next page. Make sure your subject of each sentence is the same.

Make up five sentences about the picture above using action verbs.

Sentence Structure

A complete sentence includes a subject and a verb. It expresses a complete thought. You can think about a complete sentence like a train on a track in the picture below. It leaves the tracks carrying all it's load. It completes the trip to it's destination. It has an engine and a caboose and some cargo.

A sentence fragment is like a train that forgot to take part of it's load. It forgot the cargo, it is not complete. The middle picture illustrates a run on sentence. A run-on sentence occurs when two trains are connected together, but they are not correctly attached. This train falls apart and it just runs on, missing it's destination. The third picture illustrates this.

To communicate properly, you need to write a complete sentence. Practice writing a complete sentence about a train.

The Use of It's

It's is always a contraction. There is such an animal.

Its always shows possession. There is such an animal.

Its' doesn't exist. There is no such animal!

A Narrative Paragraph

A narrative paragraph gives the details of an experience or event in story form, or in the order the events occur.

Write a paragraph of an event that has occurred recently in your life. Perhaps you were asked to sing a solo. Perhaps you lost something important and then unexpectedly found it. Read the sample paragraph. Write your own paragraph. Now use the squares to draw the events in your narrative paragraph.

    My family found something very unexpected on our weekly visit to the current river. We were having a good time floating in the cool river on our rafts when we heard barking. It almost sounded like a baby crying! Looking up, we saw an adorable poodle puppy. It was solid black and had a collar with a phone number on it's neck. We played with the puppy all afternoon and had a wonderful time. When we arrived home, we called the number. The people were very happy that their new puppy had been found and was alright. When we took the dog back, the owner handed us a ten dollar bill, enough to pay for ice cream for everyone. It was an unforgettable day at the river!

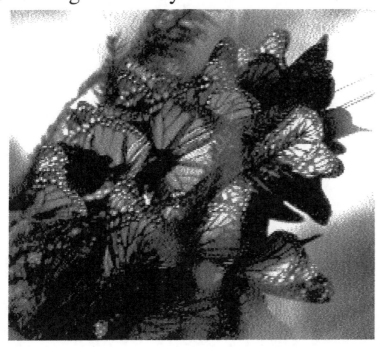

You can describe a walk you took when you saw hundreds of butterflies.

Sample Paragraphs

Descriptive:

The grove of pine trees at Paddy Creek is the most peaceful place I have ever been. The trees are tall and silent. There is no underbrush. An aroma of pine permeates the air. The only sound to be heard is a chirping bird. Paddy Creek Campground is the place I go to think.

Expository:

When making no-bake modeling dough, there is a certain procedure you must follow. First , you mix together two cups of flour, one cup of salt, and two tablespoons of vegetable oil. You also add four drops of food coloring. Now add water and knead until you have a clay consistency. You are finished! Use your clay to make a beautiful sculpture.

Persuasive:

I believe watching too much television is not good for a child's education and overall well being. Watching television takes away family time . It also takes away time from reading a good book. The morals shown on television are usually very poor. Terrible images of violence and sexual immorality abound. In conclusion, I believe television has a terrible influence on children.

Descriptive Paragraph

A descriptive paragraph describes a person, place, thing or idea. Write a descriptive paragraph about the place on this page. This place is a landscape. In a landscape, you always have an horizon line, the place where the sky and the land meet. Now draw a picture of a particular place and then describe it. This picture of the Taj Mahal is a one point perspective.

Persuasive Paragraph

A persuasive paragraph expresses an opinion and tries to convince the reader that the opinion is correct. Choose a topic about which you feel strongly. Think of a title that is very expressive of your topic. Make a poster about it.(see example) A good idea is to brainstorm on topics that people have strong feelings about. Now choose one. Remember to have a strong topic sentence with supporting information the body of the sentence. The clincher should have an an impact on the reader. The artist is saying that science has pulled the "Big Bang" theory out of a hat. Can you persuade someone with words that this might be true?

Expository Paragraph

An expository paragraph gives direction or explains something. One of the most interesting expository paragraphs I have ever read was from a student who wrote a paragraph on making elephant stew! Below is how to make an origami frog. Make one and write out the instructions.

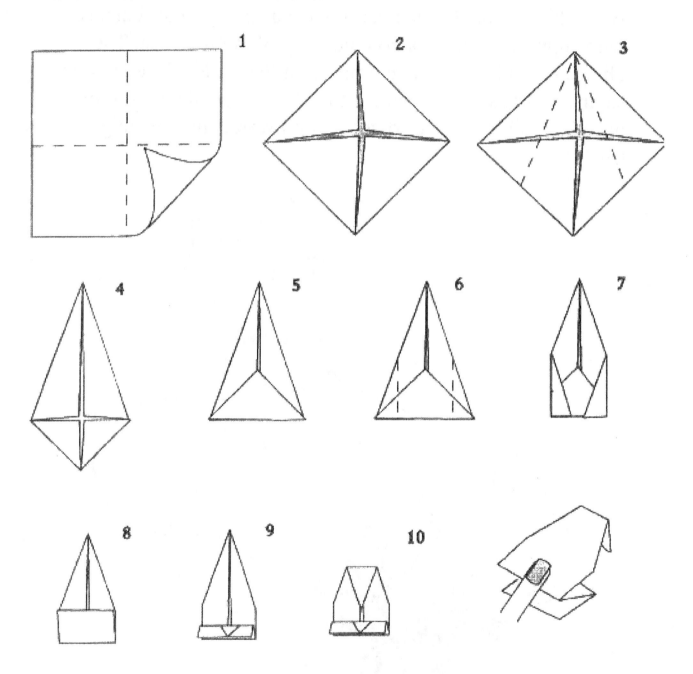

A Jumping Frog

One of Mark Twain's best short stories is called "The Celebrated Jumping Frog of Calaveras County." This is a funny story about a frog jumping contest where one of the contestants fills another contestant's frog stomach full with quail shot. What would be the result of this? Of course, the frog would not be too heavy to win the contest. If possible, read this short story by Mark Twain to the children. You could also read another favorite frog story of your own choosing.

Let's have another frog jumping contest. Origami is the technique of Japanese paper folding. On the previous page follow the simple directions on how to fold a paper frog. After the frogs are folded they can be colored with either crayons or markers. When the frogs are completed press your fingers onto the frog's back and slide it off it's rump and watch it jump!

Writing Dialogue

In learning to write dialogue, you need to remember some simple hints. It would be helpful to combine this lesson with comic strip art. Read and discuss these hints and use the comic strip blanks to create your own comic characters with dialogue. See the sample comic strip for ideas.

1. Use words that your characters would actually use if they could speak.

2. Make sure all your dialogue is meaningful.

3. Use your dialogue as people actually speak--interuptions, etc.

4. Leave some things to the reader's imagination.

5. Remember to punctuate your dialogue correctly.

6. Most of the dialogue needs to be about a character's beliefs and problems.

Biography---Autobiography

When you write the story of someone's life, you are writing a biography. When you write a story of your own life, you are writing an autobiography. Start at the beginning of your life and tell about your birth and childhood. Write how you have become what you are today. Next, draw a self-portrait of yourself from looking in a mirror, from looking in a spoon, and from memory. Put these pictures in between the pages of your autobiography . You will need to have at least two pages of writing. Use one of the self-portraits for the cover page of your autobiography.

Character Sketch

A character sketch is a short description of a person that can either stand alone or be part of a larger work. In the same way that an artist brings life to a person using a canvas and paint, a writer must bring a subject to life using pen and paper. A character sketch needs to include both physical and personal qualities of the person the sketch is about. Instead of saying that Bea is a small person, you could say that Bea is a tiny, dwarfish person with a twinkle in her eye. Look at the face below. Use your imagination and write a character sketch about this person. Now write a character sketch of your own. A great subject for a character sketch is an older person who loves to talk. Find someone who is willing to spend at least one half hour with you. Have questions prepared. Carefully observe the older person physically. Notice the surroundings of the older person. See if the person you interview will perhaps let you make a pencil sketch of their face. Write a rough draft of your character sketch first . Now allow a friend to proof it for you and make suggestions. Rewrite the character sketch in final form and allow your subject to read it and evaluate it for you!

It is said that when Leonardo da Vinci painted the *Mona Lisa* that she had recently lost a child through death. He worked very hard to get her to smile, and she would only give a half smile.

Answer these Questions

Describe the girls facial features. Are her eyes small or large? Is her hair straight or curly? Would you call her beautiful? Is there anything particularly noticeable about her clothing? What is the reason she poses with a crutch? Is her stature small or large? Describe what you imagine to be the girl's inner characteristics. Is the girl sad or happy? Would you call her a peaceful person? Do you suppose she is kind and loving, or angry and bitter? Do you suppose she cries a great deal when she is alone? Is she a very intelligent girl, or is she foolish? Open your character sketch with a topic sentence that introduces the girl. Give facts about your character in an orderly fashion, being sure to cover all aspects of her personality. Now use a good concluding sentence or summary sentence to finish your character sketch.

Caricature

A caricature is an exaggerated picture of a real person. An artist takes a person's most prominent features and exaggerates them. Look up the word <u>satire</u> in the dictionary. A caricature is a satirical picture of a person. Describe the caricature on this page. Use as many descriptive words as possible. What might be the inner qualities of this person? Choose some famous people and draw a caricature of them.

Look at this picture above. What happened in the story to get the picture above? This would be the plot of the story.

PLOT

A good story has several important elements. You need to consider setting, characters, mood, climax and plot. The plot of a story is the sequence of events. Look at the picture on the previous page . These gold prospectors are dying of starvation. A couple of men have found them. What is the sequence of events leading up to this event? Write this neatly and check for errors. When I think of a plot, I think of a map like the one below. You go on a trip, step by step, and get to a certain destination.

Climax

The whole story builds up to the climax. Look at the picture on this page and write a climax. You could set the story in the nineteenth century England. A family went to cross the ocean when their ship was hit with a whale....what happens next? In art, this would be a good picture to draw or paint. Washington Allston did many wonderful seascapes. Go to this website and describe one of them. <http://cgfa.sunsite.dk/a/p/-allston3.htm>.

Setting

The time and place of a story come together to make the setting. Look at the picture below. Write a setting for a story just from looking at the picture. Here is an example

The year was 1842. The only way to get to California was by stagecoach. Traveling in all sorts of severe weather conditions was common to the San Francisco Stage Coach LIne. It was late in December and Annie was on her way to see her long lost sister in San Fransisco. The stage coach bumped and swayed hypnotically as it lumbered up the mountain road....

Point of View

There are two kinds of point of view the student will discuss in the following picture. In the first person point of view you tell what is happening in the picture from the old man's point of view. He is telling the story and he is in the story. You might tell the story from the point of view of one of the insects he is catching. In the first person point of view you tell what is happening from the point of view of someone who is in the story. In third person point of view you tell the story from the point of view of someone outside of the story. Perhaps you want to tell the story from the point of view of a friend of a friend who knows the old man well. You tell the story from the narrator's point of view. Look at the picture of the old man catching insects at night. Tell a brief story about the picture from two different points of view.

Monologue/ A Puppet Speaks

This project is appropriate for very young children beginning with age eight to older children up to age fifteen. I have even had older students create a puppet and write a monologue and we have videotaped the performance. Look at the variety of puppets on the next page, create a puppet and write a monologue for it. A monologue is a great and grand speech given only to oneself. It could be a puppy's feelings about leaving home. It could be an assignment you give a child after you have read them a special story. Choose a character from the story and then allow them to write a story about how the character felt when......An older student can write a monologue about a famous person in history. A good topic for a monologue might be Lincoln's feelings about the Civil War. I had some eighth grade students write a puppet play about children being kind to one another. When children can hear how sad someone feels when something unkind is said, it helps them to be more sensitive.

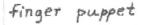

finger puppet

Cut basic shape

glue in cone shape

ADD YARN AND PAPER

mouse

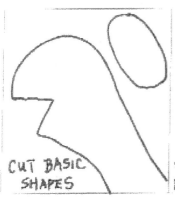

CUT BASIC SHAPES

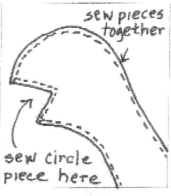

sew pieces together

sew circle piece here

decorate puppet

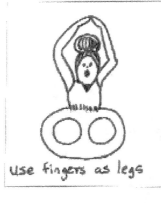

use fingers as legs

BASIC CARDBOARD SHAPE

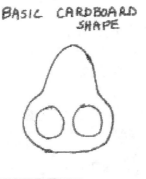

SMALL BROWN PAPER BAG

DECORATE

INDEX CARD

DECORATE

Writing an Ending

The ending of a story is very important. This is the last page in a story about a tortoise and a hare. The artist wants you to write an ending for the story. Use your imagination and write the ending of the story. What lesson can people learn from this story?

Understanding Communications

Editorials, news writing, and propaganda are all important to the understanding of communications. Children need to understand that people are communicating with them on a daily basis in visual and written ways. Discuss how commercials, billboards, newspapers, and magazines form our opinion on a variety of topics. In the book title below, the artist wanted to convey that the book is called Master Drawing, but he also wanted a picture of Christ as the master in the title so people would understand it was a Christian drawing program. Do you think he was effec-

Making an Outline

An outline is a guide that will help you as you write. It is an organized list of how your essay will progress. Look at the picture on the next page. What is the artist saying about television? He saying that he believes television eats your time and that it throws up garbage on you. Do you agree with that? Write an essay on television from this outline.

Subject: Television

Topic: Do you believe it is good or bad?

I. Reason one
  A. Supporting detail
    1. Specific example
    2. Specific example
  B. Supporting detail
    1. Specific example
    2. Specific example

II. Reason two
  A. Supporting detail
    1. Specific example
    2. Specific example
  B. Supporting detail
    1. Specific example
    2. Specific example

III. Conclusion

Write this essay in complete form. Make it one to two pages long. Did having an outline make it easier?

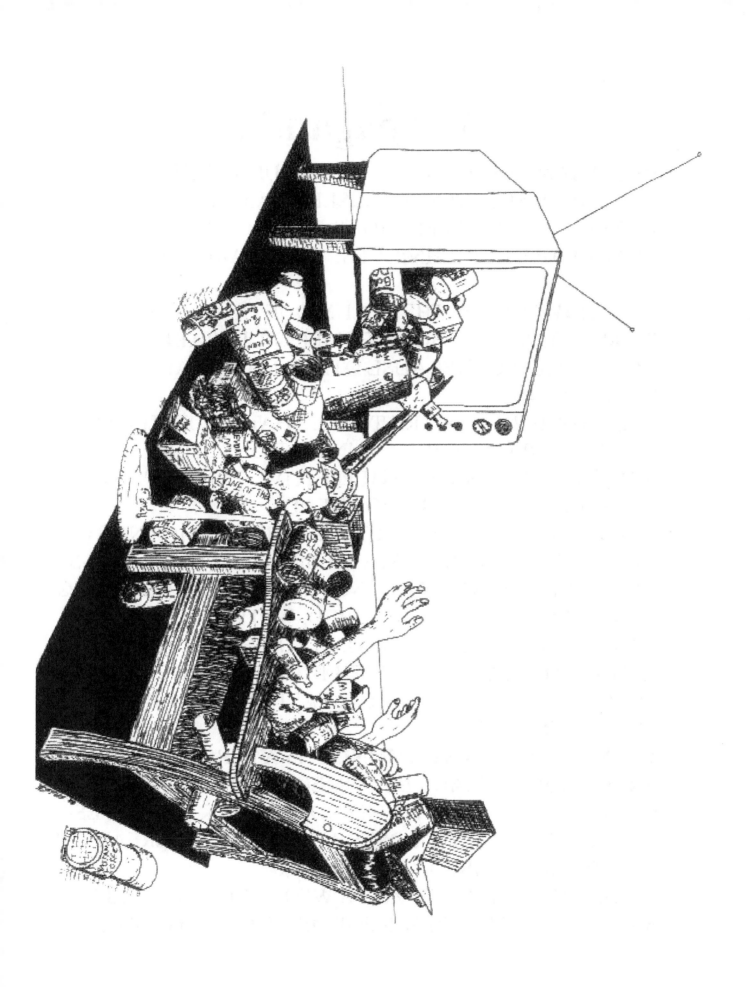

Propaganda

PROPAGANDA IS USED BY A COMMUNICATOR (A WRITER OR SPEAKER) TO MISLEAD AN AUDIENCE BY APPEALING TO ITS EMOTIONS. FOLLOWING ARE SEVERAL COMMON TECHNIQUES. THERE ARE MANY OTHERS.

1. **BANDWAGON** IS THE TECHNIQUE OF PRESSURING PEOPLE TO ACCEPT SOME BELIEF OR TO TAKE SOME ACTION MERELY BECAUSE OTHER PEOPLE ARE DOING SO. (A POLL)

2. **LOADED WORDS** ARE THOSE THAT HAVE STRONG POSITIVE OR NEGATIVE CONNOTATIONS. PURR WORDS ARE LOADED WORDS WITH POSITIVE CONNOTATIONS, SUCH AS DUMB, WEAK, HOT-HEAD.

3. **TRANSFER** IS THE TECHNIQUE OF ATTEMPTING TO GET PEOPLE TO ASSOCIATE THEIR POSITIVE FEELINGS ABOUT ONE THING WITH ANOTHER UNRELATED THING. AN ADVERTISER WHO USES RED, WHITE, AND BLUE BANNERS MAY BE ATTEMPTING TO GET PEOPLE TO ASSOCIATE PATRIOTISM WITH BUYING PARTICULAR PRODUCTS.)(SELLING BREAKFAST CEREAL ABOUT A TELEVISION SHOW?)

4. **UNRELIABLE TESTIMONIAL** IS A PERSONAL ENDORSEMENT MADE BY SOMEONE WHO IS NOT QUALIFIED TO MAKE THE ENDORSEMENT. (A PROFESSIONAL ATHLETE ENDORSES A BREAKFAST CEREAL -- IS HE A NUTRITIONIST?)

LOOK THROUGH MAGAZINES WITH YOUR CHILDREN AND POINT OUT VARIOUS FORMS OF PROPAGANDA.

LOADED WORDS

LOADED WORDS HAVE STRONG POSITIVE OR NEGATIVE CONNOTATIONS. PURR WORDS ARE LOADED WITH POSITIVE CONNOTATIONS. SNARL WORDS HAVE NEGATIVE CONNOTATIONS. IF YOU ARE TRYING TO CONVINCE SOMEONE THAT SOMETHING IS GOOD, YOU MUST USE MANY PURR WORDS. AT ELECTION TIME, YOU CAN BE SURE THAT CAMPAIGN MANAGERS ARE CAREFUL TO USE MANY PURR WORDS ABOUT THEIR CANDIDATE AND MANY SNARL WORDS ABOUT THE CANDIDATE THAT THEY ARE RUNNING AGAINST. WORDS CAN HAVE GREAT POWER TO SWAY OPINION. CHOOSE A PLACE IN THE WORLD. YOU HAVE BEEN CHOSEN TO BE THE ADVERTISING AGENCY TO PROMOTE THIS PLACE. MAKE A BROCHURE TO SEND TO CONVINCE PEOPLE TO COME TO THIS PLACE. USE AS MANY PURR WORDS AS POSSIBLE. MAKE SURE THE BROCHURE IS COMPLETE WITH PICTURES.

TRANSFER

TRANSFER IS THE ATTEMPT TO GET PEOPLE TO ASSOCIATE THEIR POSITIVE FEELINGS ABOUT ONE THING WITH ANOTHER RELATED THING. YOU MIGHT USE RED, WHITE, AND BLUE TO SELL HOUSE PAINT. PEOPLE WOULD SEE THE BACKGROUND AND HAVE A POSITIVE FEELING ABOUT YOUR PRODUCT. YOU MIGHT USE THE SYMBOL OF THE RINGS OF THE OLYMPICS TO SELL TENNIS SHOES. PEOPLE USE THIS TECHNIQUE TO SELL PRODUCTS AND IDEAS.

UNRELIABLE TESTIMONIAL

UNRELIABLE TESTIMONIAL IS A PERSONAL ENDORSEMENT MADE BY SOMEONE WHO IS NOT QUALIFIED TO MAKE THE ENDORSEMENT. A PROFESSIONAL ATHLETE ENDORSES A BREAKFAST CEREAL -- IS HE A NUTRITIONIST?

I think Checkmate soccer balls are the best.

BANDWAGON

BANDWAGON IS THE TECHNIQUE OF PRESSURING PEOPLE TO ACCEPT SOME BELIEF OR TO TAKE SOME ACTION MERELY BECAUSE OTHER PEOPLE ARE DOING SO. "EVERYBODY'S DOING IT, SO YOU NEED TO, TOO." DECIDE ON A TYPE OF CEREAL YOU ARE MARKETING. NOW DESIGN THE FRONT OF THE BOX USING THE BANDWAGON TYPE OF PROPAGANDA. :"IT'S EVERYONE'S FAVORITE!!" "100% OF THE PEOPLE USE _____YOU NEED IT TOO."

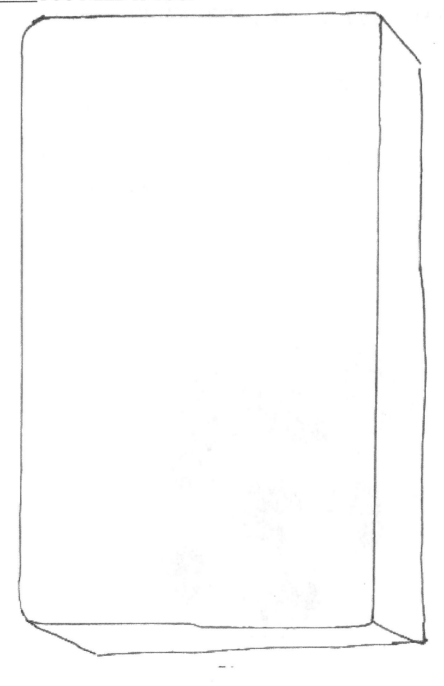

Whales Are in the News

Studying and writing newspaper articles is a lot of fun. Choose a topic that interests you. Whales are in the news. Research information on whales. A good topic sentence for a news article will give you certain information. It will generally answer the 5 W's. What is that? The five W's are **who, what, when, where,** and **why**. Can you answer all these questions in one sentence? Willy the whale's owners found out that on September 5, 1995 he would have to move his home to another aquarium because of state regulations. Write a newspaper article about whales. Look up Miller and Nelson, well known ocean artists, on the internet. Copy one of their whale pictures to go with your story.

WRITING AN EDITORIAL

AN EDITORIAL'S PRIMARY PURPOSE IS TO INFLU-
ENCE ITS READERS TO ONE OPINION OR ANOTHER.
HOWEVER, IT CAN ALSO INFORM, PROMOTE AN
IDEA, PRAISE INDIVIDUALS OR EVENTS, AND EVEN
ENTERTAIN. GO TO THE EDITORIAL PAGE OF YOUR
LOCAL NEWSPAPER. PERHAPS, IF YOU ARE FROM A
SMALL TOWN, YOU WILL WANT TO GO TO THE EDI-
TORIAL PAGE OF A LARGE METROPOLITAN (CITY)
NEWSPAPER. READ SOME EDITORIALS CAREFULLY.
WHAT PURPOSE DO YOU SUPPOSE THE WRITER HAD
IN DOING THE EDITORIAL? WERE YOU INFLUENCED
ONE WAY OR ANOTHER? NOW LOOK AT THE POLITI-
CAL CARTOONS. IT IS SAID A PICTURE IS WORTH A
THOUSAND WORDS.   WERE YOU INFLUENCED BY
THE PICTURE? THE ASSIGNMENT IS TO TAKE A
TOPIC AND WRITE AN EDITORIAL ABOUT IT. MAKE
SURE YOU ARE SIMPLE AND DIRECT. TRY NOT TO
BE TOO DRAMATIC. NOW DRAW A POLITICAL CAR-
TOON ABOUT THE SAME TOPIC YOU WRITE ON.
WHICH WAY DO YOU BELIEVE WORKED THE BEST
IN COMMUNICATING YOUR IDEA. DRAW YOUR
POLITICAL CARTOON IN PENCIL FIRST, THEN GO
OVER IT IN INK AND SEND IT TO YOUR LOCAL
PAPER.

Thomas Nast, one of the most famous political car-
toonists in history, invented the Republican elephant and
the Democratic donkey.

Letters

First, design a special letterhead for your letter. Look at various letterhead ideas. See the sample letterhead below. Take a plain piece of paper and lightly pencil in the information you want to include on the letterhead. Go over your design with colored ink pens. If you want to reproduce your design, it may photocopy easier if you use a black ink pen. Your finished design may even become your family logo. It is important to know correct letter form. Go to this web site for information on how to write letters. The assignment is to write a friendly letter of appreciation to someone who has been very special in your life. It needs to be someone you know personally. Next, write a letter in business form to someone you appreciate that you do not know. This might be a senator, your pastor, or a sports figure. In both assignments, the letter needs to express your feelings. Go to this website for information<http://depts.gallaudex.edu/english-works/writing/main/letter.htm>.

Poetry

Poetry is using words to express ideas or pictures. Look at the haiku poem below. A haiku poem is a Japanese form of poetry that presents a picture in nature. There are 5 syllables in the first line, 7 syllables in the second line and 5 syllables in the third line. Look at the picture at the bottom of the page. Did the poet capture the image?

Silent lily pads

Turtles playing hide and seek

In the flower pond

Concrete Poetry

Concrete poetry is where the poem takes the shape of what the poem is about. Write a poem about a roller coaster.

My elephant is HUGE...

He uses his trunk to sway back and forth back and forth

He sways so gently......back and forth....my elephant.

Writers and Poets as Artists

Literary figures such as O. Henry, Robert Lewis Stevenson, Oscar Wilde were also wonderful artists. Illustrate in a picture one of the poems below.

Emily Bronte wrote,
What through the stars and fair moonlight
Are quenched in moonlight dull and gray? They are but tokens of the night, and this my soul is day.

Edgar Allan Poe, great writer of the epic rhyme "The Raven," was a wonderful portrait artist. His parents owned a pencil factory.

E.E. Cummings, an excellent artist, one of the most famous poets in American history, famous for his free verse wrote,
Why do you paint?
For exactly the same reason that I breathe.
That's not an answer.
There isn't any answer.
How long hasn't there been any answer?
As long as I can remember, I mean poetry
So do I.
Tell me, doesn't your painting interfere with your writing?
Quite the contrary, they love each other dearly.

One of the greatest portions of English Literature is Macbeth's words,
Life's but a walking shadow, a poor player
That struts and frets his hour on the stage and then is heard no more
It is a tale told by an idiot, full of sound and fury,
signifying nothing.

Rudyard Kipling

Here is a poem and a drawing by Rudyard Kilpling:

When the flush of a newborn sun fell first on Eden's green and gold,
Our father Adam sat under the tree and scratched with a stick in the mould;
and the first rude sketch that the world had seen was joy to his mighty heart,
Till the Devil whispered behind the leaves, it's pretty but is it art?

Sometimes we think this about modern art. Below is a copy of a boat drawn by Kipling. Write a poem and draw a picture of it.

Telling a Story in Three Ways

The story <u>The Lion, the Witch and the Wardrobe</u> by C. S. Lewis in in three different forms. It can be read as a book. It can be listened to from a CD or tape. Finally, it can be watched and listened to as a movie or cartoon. We have both in our home. Artists bring a story to life visually. You can make an Aslan wanted poster. There are many art projects that are very enjoyable associated with this story. Use the directions below to make a throne for either Peter, Lucy, Susan or Edward. Describe what the throne will look like in words first. Then build what you have described. Paper needs to be at least 80 pound. Use feathers, sparkles, glue scissors, tissue paper, etc.

Rebus

A rebus was very popular in early American classrooms. This is a representation of words using symbols, pictures, letters and numbers whose names look like the word being written. If you were writing the word stop using a rebus, you would draw a picture of a top and put S+ in front of it. Look at the Rebus below and make your own.

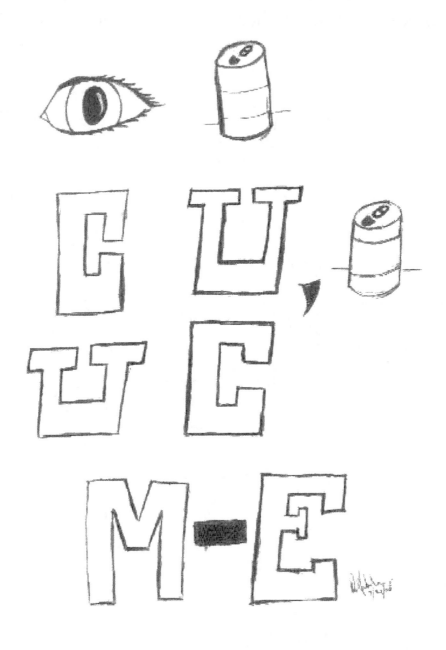

Albert Einstein

Albert Einstein was one of the greatest scientists of all time. In the *Einstein Papers* of 1905 he made three of his greatest contributions to scientific thought. Each of the papers became the start of a new branch of physics. He is best know for the famous equation $E=MC_2$ He stated, **"In the middle of every difficulty lies opportunity."** Many times great inventors have many failures before they succeed at an invention. Edison failed over 1000 times when inventing the light bulb. Write a paragraph on why this statement is important to understanding Einstein. Draw Einstein using the grid.

Franklin Roosevelt

Franklin Roosevelt was one of our truly great presidents. He was the thirty-second President of the United States. The last words he wrote on the day of his death were, **"The only limit to our realization of tomorrow will be our doubts of today. Let us move forward with strong and active faith."** What happened to him in 1921 that would change his life forever? When you have discovered this by researching on the internet, answer this question. Do you believe that overcoming great odds in a positive way is an important attribute of someone who is a leader? Draw Roosevelt using the grid.

Helen Keller

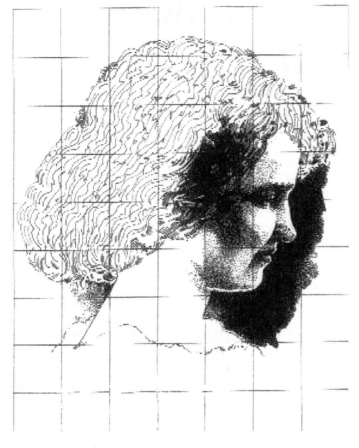

Helen Keller's life was filled with triumph. Although she could not speak or hear, she greatly influenced all around her. She especially encouraged other handicapped people to make the most of what God had given them. She learned to speak and read braille and went to Radcliff college and graduated with honors. She appeared before legislatures and gave lectures and wrote books. She said," **I am only one: But still I am one. I cannot do everything, but still I can do something, and because I cannot do everything, I will not refuse to do something that I can do."** Use your reference books and look up the name of the person who was Helen Keller's teacher. Write about the size of the part her teacher had in her great success.
Draw Helen Keller using the grid.

Teddy Roosevelt

Teddy Roosevelt, the twenty-sixth President of the United States had the saying attributed to him, **"Speak softly and carry a big stick."** What do you think this might mean for an individual and then for a country? Teddy lost his young wife and his mother within a short period of time. The tragedy convinced him to go out west. He said, **"The credit belongs to the man who is actually in the arena, who strives valiantly; who knows the great enthusiasm, the great devotions and spends himself in a worthy cause; who at the best, knows the triumph of high achievements and who, at the worst, if he fails, at least fails while daring greatly, so that his place shall never be with those cold and timid souls who know neither victory or defeat."** Write a character sketch about Teddy Roosevelt. Draw him using the grid.

Winston Churchill

Winston Churchill did poorly in his early studies. He did not enter formal school until he was twelve, when he entered Harrow School, a leading English secondary school. He was always the lowest boy in the lowest class and yet in 1953 he won the Noble Prize for literature. He is considered one of the greatest statesmen in world history. Upon becoming Prime Minister of Great Britain, Winston said, **"I felt as if I were walking with destiny, and that all my past life had been but a preparation for this hour and for this trial."** Churchill was Prime Minister of Great Britain in what year? Do you believe God prepares us for what he leads us to do? Write a persuasive paragraph about what you believe about his. Draw Churchill using the grid.

IZZIE

Carol Hubal wrote this delightful rhyming poem about *Izzie's Soup Kitchen.* Go to this website to learn more about kinds of rhymes: <http://en.wikipedia.org/wiki/Rhyme>.

It's a great day for soup! said Izzie to Drew
Let's get out the kettle and chopping block, too
We'll make a big pot and invite folks to eat
We'll throw in all veggies and skip any meat
They'll be cabbage, potatoes, tomatoes and beans, Corn,
rutabagas, and all kinds of greens

Add six lines to this poem, making sure they all rhyme.

The Jungle Book

<u>The Jungle Book</u> by Rudyard Kipling is timeless in its popularity. There are several animated versions and at least two movie versions of the story. Have children read this book in its original written form, then let them watch a film or animated version and then compare. Have them make the art project below and tell how they did it. Let them choose an incident from the book and tell it from the animal's perspective. They will need construction paper and towel rolls and paper plates, glue, etc.

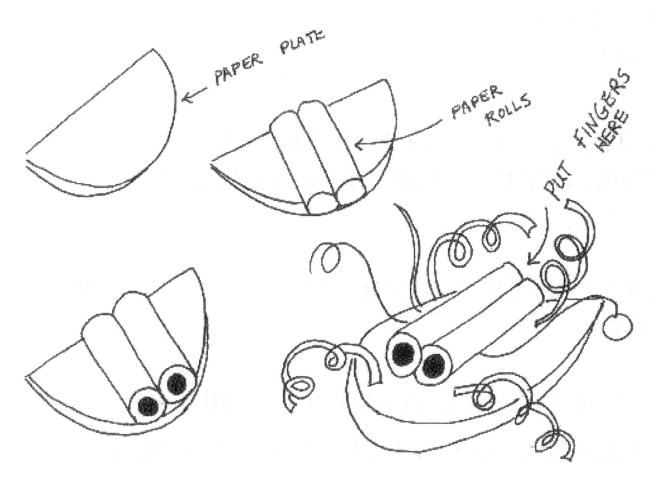

DECORATE YOUR
BUG HEAD WITH SUPPLIES
OF YOUR CHOICE

BOOK REPORT FORM

BOOK TITLE-

BOOK AUTHOR-

MAIN CHARACTERS-

SETTING-
PLOT-

If THE BOOK IS NONFICTION, NAME THE PRIMARY IDEAS SET FORTH IN THE BOOK.

DID YOU LIKE THE BOOK? WHY OR WHY NOT?

LOOK AT THE COVER OF THE BOOK.
DESIGN A NEW COVER FOR THE BOOK.

Expository Paragraph

A wonderful idea for an expository paragraph is to go to the following website first; <earth.google.com>. You can type in any place in the world including someone's address and get a picture of where they are in relation to the earth, their country, their city and their neighborhood. Type in the Great Pyramids first. Go there and explain what you see and how others can do this. Write your paragraph in the space below. Draw the picture of the pyramids below. Where is the light coming from? Make sure you shade the picture correctly.

_____

_____

_____

_____

_____

_____

_____

_____

_____

_____

_____

Persuasive Paragraph

Charles Dickens was one of the most famous of the English novelists. He wrote fifteen novels and created many distinctive characters. At the age of ten he went to work in a factory warehouse. Situations and characters in his books convinced many readers that something had to be done about the work conditions of children. The book <u>David Copperfield</u> is about his own experiences in the workhouse. Write a persuasive paragraph to go with the pictures below.

_____
_____
_____
_____
_____
_____
_____
_____
_____
_____
_____
_____
_____
_____
_____
_____
_____
_____

Descriptive Paragraph

Write a descriptive paragraph of the scene above.

_____

_____

_____

_____

_____

_____

_____

_____

Narrative Paragraph

Write your narrative paragraph here. What is happening?

_____

_____

_____

_____

_____

_____

Check sheet for Producing a Video

1. Brainstorm for an idea.

2. Outline major points.

3. Focus on a message to communicate.

4. Write effective opening.

5. Write effective closing, summarizing the message of the video.

6. Create your dialogue.

7. Designate someone to run the camcorder and direct the action.

8. Practice your presentation; make needed changes.

9. Evaluate success of your production.
For a great site on writing a storyboard:
http://www.storycenter.org/memvoice/pages/tutorial_3.html

Bye
Folks!

MORE BOOKS FROM VISUAL MANNA

***Art Through the Core* series...**

    Teaching American History Through Art
    Teaching Astronomy Through Art
    Teaching English Through Art
    Teaching History Through Art
    Teaching Literature Through Art
    Teaching Math Through Art
    Teaching Science Through Art
    Teaching Social Studies Through Art

Other Books...

    Art Adventures in Narnia
    Art Basics for Children
    Bible Arts & Crafts
    Christian Holiday Arts & Crafts
    Dragons, Dinosaurs, Castles and Knights
    Drawing, Painting and Sculpting Horses
    Expanding Your Horizons Through Words
    Indians In Art
    Master Drawing
    Preschool & Early Elementary Art Basics
    Preschool Bible Lessons
    Visual Manna 1: Complete Art Curriculum
    Visual Manna 2: Advanced Techniques

Books available at Rainbow Resource Center:
www.rainbowresource.com • 888.841.3456

VISUAL | MANNA

Educating with art since 1992!

A Christian is one whose imagination should fly beyond the stars. Francis Schaeffer

His Lions

Contact *visualmanna@gmail.com* if you are interested in our Intern program. Students learn how to teach art, do murals for ministry, prepare an excellent portfolio, and much more. Go to **visualmanna.com** for information.

Free art lessons are available at **OurHomeschoolForum.com** and books are available at Rainbow Resource Center (**www.rainbowresource.com**). Try all our "Art Through the Core" series and other books as well! Make learning fun for kids!!! Sharon Jeffus teaches Art Intensives in person for the Landry Academy at **landryacademy.com**.